If you have purchased this Diary/Journal without its cover, it may be a stolen book. Neither the publisher or the author is under any obligation to provide professional services in anyway, legal, health or in any form which is related to this book, its contents advice or otherwise.

The law and practices vary from country to country and state to state.

If legal or professional information is required, the purchaser, or the reader should seek the information privately and best suited to their particular needs, and circumstances.

The author and publisher specifically disclaim any liability that may be incurred from the information within this book.

All rights reserved. No part of this book, including the interior design, images, cover design, diagrams, or any intellectual property (IP), icons and photographs may be reproduced or transmitted in any form by any means (electronic, photocopying, recording or otherwise) without the prior permission of the publisher. ©

Copyright© 2023 MSI Australia

All rights reserved.

ISBN: 978-0-6459403-0-5

Published by How2Books
Under licence from MSI Ltd, Australia
Company Registration No: 96963518255
NSW, Australia

See our website: www.how2books.com.au
Or contact by email: sales@how2books.com.au
Covers and Copyright owned by MSI, Australia

MSI acknowledges the author and images, text and photographs used in this book.

Published by How2Books

10% of the sale of each book helps to support Diabetes Type One and Cancer Research.

The Magic of Chelsea

YOUR DIARY/JOURNAL

*A single, white flag iris,
Nature's Perfection...*

An arrangement of double fern-leaf peony flowers, raffia wrapped twine threading its way through the design, smaller placements of lavender to purple flowers, and the use of the Hogarth Curve in the flowing lines; giving an overall combination which was breathtaking.

JANUARY

1)	Monday
2)	Tuesday
3)	Wednesday
4)	Thursday

JANUARY

5)	Friday
6)	Saturday
7)	Sunday
8)	Monday

JANUARY

9)	Tuesday
10)	Wednesday
11)	Thursday
12)	Friday

JANUARY

13)	Saturday
14)	Sunday
15)	Monday
16)	Tuesday

JANUARY

17) Wednesday

18) Thursday

19) Friday

20) Saturday

JANUARY

21)	Sunday

22)	Monday

23)	Tuesday

24)	Wednesday

JANUARY

25)	Thursday
26)	Friday
27)	Saturday
28)	Sunday

JANUARY

29)	Monday
30)	Tuesday
31)	Wednesday

Your Notes
....
....
....
....

Ivy geranium is always a great asset whether grown in the garden or flowerpot.

A single and perfectly unfurling, David Austin Rose, seen in the rose garden at the Chelsea Flower Show.

FEBRUARY

1)	Thursday
2)	Friday
3)	Saturday
4)	Sunday

FEBRUARY

5) Monday

6) Tuesday

7) Wednesday

8) Thursday

FEBRUARY

9)	Friday
10)	Saturday
11)	Sunday
12)	Monday

FEBRUARY

13) Tuesday

14) Wednesday

15) Thursday

16) Friday

FEBRUARY

17) Saturday
18) Sunday
19) Monday
20) Tuesday

FEBRUARY

21)	Wednesday
22)	Thursday
23)	Friday
24)	Saturday

FEBRUARY

25) Sunday

26) Monday

27) Tuesday

28) Wednesday

29) Thursday

Your Notes
....
....
....

Double-flowering Oriental Lilies with perfume of opulence and a stunning display. The pink tinged edge gives an almost 'candy rock' appearance to these beautiful blooms.

Cascades of flowing white phalaenopsis orchids, white allium, and what appears to be long rolls of natural cotton, white arum lilies, and plumosus asparagus fern are used in this large basket flower arrangement.

The colour of the iris flowers this year at the show, were beyond beautiful, just magnificent to see the range of colours on offer with new colours being developed...!

MARCH

1) Friday

2) Saturday

3) Sunday

4) Monday

MARCH

5)	Tuesday
6)	Wednesday
7)	Thursday
8)	Friday

MARCH

9) Saturday

10) Sunday

11) Monday

12) Tuesday

MARCH

13) Wednesday

14) Thursday

15) Friday

16) Saturday

MARCH

17) Sunday
18) Monday
19) Tuesday
20) Wednesday

MARCH

21)	Thursday
22)	Friday
23)	Saturday
24)	Sunday

MARCH

25) Monday
26) Tuesday
27) Wednesday
28) Thursday

MARCH

29)	Friday

30)	Saturday

31)	Sunday

Your Notes
....
....
....
....

Chelsea 'GOLD'. 'The Beauty of Recycling', this arrangement, as you can see, is of the colours: lilacs, lavender and purple, with just a touch of chartreuse; thus, a combination of peace and stillness with using colour! With so many of the cut flowers sitting in singular bottles, the design will remain fresh for many days; this is a new approach to floristry.

There were masses of colour, vibrance and energy seen in the Trinidad and Tobago floral exhibits.

APRIL

1)	Monday
2)	Tuesday
3)	Wednesday
4)	Thursday

APRIL

5) Friday

6) Saturday

7) Sunday

8) Monday

APRIL

9)	Tuesday
10)	Wednesday
11)	Thursday
12)	Friday

APRIL

13) Saturday

14) Sunday

15) Monday

16) Tuesday

APRIL

17) Wednesday
18) Thursday
19) Friday
20) Saturday

APRIL

21)	Sunday
22)	Monday
23)	Tuesday
24)	Wednesday

APRIL

25) Thursday
26) Friday
27) Saturday
28) Sunday

APRIL

29) Monday

30) Tuesday

Your Notes
....
....
....
....
....
....
....
....
....

The iris flower, originally found in Syria in 1469 BC by king Thutmose lll. He liked the flower so much; he took the bulbs back to Egypt where it became a beloved flower of the Egyptians.

We now see the beautiful blooms in many parts of the world, including in great displays, as we see in the above.

'Use and recycle' were the directions given to the floristry exhibitors at Chelsea this year, and full use of metal drums was made abundant in the displays by florists and floral artists.

MAY

1)	Wednesday
2)	Thursday
3)	Friday
4)	Saturday

MAY

5)	Sunday

6)	Monday

7)	Tuesday

8)	Wednesday

MAY

9)	Thursday
10)	Friday
11)	Saturday
12)	Sunday

MAY

13) Monday

14) Tuesday

15) Wednesday

16) Thursday

MAY

17)	Friday
18)	Saturday
19)	Sunday
20)	Monday

MAY

21)	Tuesday
22)	Wednesday
23)	Thursday
24)	Friday

MAY

25)	Saturday

26)	Sunday

27)	Monday

28)	Tuesday

MAY

29)	Wednesday
30)	Thursday
31)	Friday

Your Notes

....
....
....
....
....

From cascading orchids of many varieties to new techniques in plant adaption and growing, all was on show at this year's Show.

Cymbidium orchids are seen in the above photograph.

Gladiolus, after many years of being out of favour with the public; as a cut flower, it is slowly making a comeback!

This flower offers many different colours and is a great asset in both modern and traditional flower designs.

JUNE

1)	Saturday
2)	Sunday
3)	Monday
4)	Tuesday

JUNE

5) Wednesday

6) Thursday

7) Friday

8) Saturday

JUNE

9)	Sunday
10)	Monday
11)	Tuesday
12)	Wednesday

JUNE

13)	Thursday
14)	Friday
15)	Saturday
16)	Sunday

JUNE

17) Monday

18) Tuesday

19) Wednesday

20) Thursday

JUNE

21)	Friday
22)	Saturday
23)	Sunday
24)	Monday

JUNE

25) Tuesday
26) Wednesday
27) Thursday
28) Friday

JUNE

29)	Saturday
30)	Sunday

Your Notes

....
....
....
....
....
....
....
....
....
....

Disbud chrysanthemums were originally cultivated in China in the 15th Century BC. In the 21st Century, these flowers now have a royal attachment to Japan and are part of the Imperial Seal of that country.

They are a truly magnificent flower.

*Zantedeschia –
Colours to Make Your Heart Sing...*

With so many tantalising colours, these flowers offer their beauty in both modern and traditional flower arrangements, and as house decoration flowers and plants.

JULY

1)	Monday
2)	Tuesday
3)	Wednesday
4)	Thursday

JULY

5) Friday

6) Saturday

7) Sunday

8) Monday

JULY

9)	Tuesday
10)	Wednesday
11)	Thursday
12)	Friday

JULY

13)	Saturday
14)	Sunday
15)	Monday
16)	Tuesday

JULY

17) Wednesday

18) Thursday

19) Friday

20) Saturday

JULY

21)	Sunday
22)	Monday
23)	Tuesday
24)	Wednesday

JULY

25) Thursday
26) Friday
27) Saturday
28) Sunday

JULY

29)	Monday
30)	Tuesday
31)	Wednesday

Your Notes

....
....
....
....
....

The Mush Room

This stand wins 'GOLD'.
Human creativity and skill, and a great deal of knowledge, has developed these different mushrooms which are not only edible but also used as features in many venues, which in themselves, create talking points.

The freshness and vibrancy of this beautiful narcissus cannot be denied.

From the three uniquely shaped inside petals, to the outer shape, was breathtaking.

Narcissus and daffodils do have a soft, delicate perfume, and once associated with the human senses, the perfume works its own soothing qualities on the human system.

AUGUST

1)	Thursday
2)	Friday
3)	Saturday
4)	Sunday

AUGUST

5) Monday

6) Tuesday

7) Wednesday

8) Thursday

AUGUST

9)	Friday
10)	Saturday
11)	Sunday
12)	Monday

AUGUST

13) Tuesday

14) Wednesday

15) Thursday

16) Friday

AUGUST

17) Saturday
18) Sunday
19) Monday
20) Tuesday

AUGUST

21)	Wednesday
22)	Thursday
23)	Friday
24)	Saturday

AUGUST

25)	Sunday
26)	Monday
27)	Tuesday
28)	Wednesday

AUGUST

29)	Thursday
30)	Friday
31)	Saturday

Your Notes
....
....
....
....

Magnificent delphiniums and begonias in contrasting colours, a splendid display...

It is the dedication by the growers to the blooms shown at Chelsea that gives the audience the remarkable displays we see. The delphinium and begonias were exquisite in their appearance.

The pair of flower arrangements in the above photograph are of the 'Hogarth Curve' and are seen in contrasting colour combinations. Each pair has a matching arrangement which gives the design a three-dimensional perspective.

Please look closely and you will see, there are not two arrangements in the above, but four...!

SEPTEMBER

1)	Sunday
2)	Monday
3)	Tuesday
4)	Wednesday

SEPTEMBER

5)	Thursday
6)	Friday
7)	Saturday
8)	Sunday

SEPTEMBER

9)	Monday
10)	Tuesday
11)	Wednesday
12)	Thursday

SEPTEMBER

13)	Friday
14)	Saturday
15)	Sunday
16)	Monday

SEPTEMBER

17) Tuesday
18) Wednesday
19) Thursday
20) Friday

SEPTEMBER

21) Saturday

22) Sunday

23) Monday

24) Tuesday

SEPTEMBER

25) Wednesday

26) Thursday

27) Friday

28) Saturday

SEPTEMBER

29)	Sunday
30)	Monday

Your Notes
....
....
....
....
....
....
....
....
....

Singular beauty seen in a mass display of clematis. In the above photograph, this new cultivar named the Duchess of Wessex, displayed a magnificent show of fine flowers.

This variety had a soft, but delicious scent and created a soothing combination within such a busy location.

Another Reign Begins...

Looking closely, you will see, this whole design is made from dried vine and wispy dried tree branches...

This is a very large masterpiece when compared to the gentleman in the photograph...!

OCTOBER

1)	Tuesday
2)	Wednesday
3)	Thursday
4)	Friday

OCTOBER

5) Saturday

6) Sunday

7) Monday

8) Tuesday

OCTOBER

9)	Wednesday
10)	Thursday
11)	Friday
12)	Saturday

OCTOBER

13) Sunday

14) Monday

15) Tuesday

16) Wednesday

OCTOBER

17) Thursday
18) Friday
19) Saturday
20) Sunday

OCTOBER

21) Monday

22) Tuesday

23) Wednesday

24) Thursday

OCTOBER

25)	Friday
26)	Saturday
27)	Sunday
28)	Monday

OCTOBER

29)	Tuesday

30)	Wednesday

31)	Thursday

Your Notes
....
....
....
....

The European Peony flower, and what a spectacle it was to see, with the petals so fragile, they equal the wings of a summer butterfly...? This truly simple, cleverly constructed by nature, is beautiful and a gentle flower. It has the pureness of colour and was exceptional to see.

An Ikebana Master...

In the above photograph, we see the trueness of culture, control, and creativity.

The use of the new shoots within the maple branch placements, the strength of the line from what may be a gladiolus, sword shaped leaf, the use of a full flower iris and the iris buds, with a placement of hydrangea stem complete with new buds and fresh leaves, then the placement of one yellow wildflower daisy all adds to the rhythm of this design.

NOVEMBER

1)	Friday
2)	Saturday
3)	Sunday
4)	Monday

NOVEMBER

5) Tuesday

6) Wednesday

7) Thursday

8) Friday

NOVEMBER

9) Saturday

10) Sunday

11) Monday

12) Tuesday

NOVEMBER

13)	Wednesday

14)	Thursday

15)	Friday

16)	Saturday

NOVEMBER

17) Sunday

18) Monday

19) Tuesday

20) Wednesday

NOVEMBER

21) Thursday

22) Friday

23) Saturday

24) Sunday

NOVEMBER

25)	Monday
26)	Tuesday
27)	Wednesday
28)	Thursday

NOVEMBER

29) Friday

30) Saturday

Your Notes
....
....
....
....
....
....
....
....
....

There was such an abundance of these beautiful flowers at the show, the perfume filled the air, and the visual sight was breathtaking...

![Alliums display photograph]

Alliums were very popular; many are now being used in the commercial flower industry in floral design work, while many flower arrangers also like the difference the shape brings to their designs….

In the above, alliums from the massed heads, to the lightly, almost 'spider like' flowers at the forefront of the photograph.

DECEMBER

1)	Sunday
2)	Monday
3)	Tuesday
4)	Wednesday

DECEMBER

5)	Thursday
6)	Friday
7)	Saturday
8)	Sunday

DECEMBER

9)	Monday
10)	Tuesday
11)	Wednesday
12)	Thursday

DECEMBER

13)	Friday
14)	Saturday
15)	Sunday
16)	Monday

DECEMBER

17)	Tuesday
18)	Wednesday
19)	Thursday
20)	Friday

DECEMBER

21) Saturday

22) Sunday

23) Monday

24) Tuesday

DECEMBER

25)	Wednesday
26)	Thursday
27)	Friday
28)	Saturday

DECEMBER

29)	Sunday

30)	Monday

31)	Tuesday

Your Notes

Your Notes

The Magic of Chelsea

www.ingramcontent.com/pod-product-compliance
Lightning Source LLC
Chambersburg PA
CBHW051539010526
44107CB00064B/2777